Dedication

To all the readers.

Uncolored Thoughts

Dr. Sulabh Kumar Shrestha

Published by quillyporcupine, 2023.

While every precaution has been taken in the preparation of this book, the publisher assumes no responsibility for errors or omissions, or for damages resulting from the use of the information contained herein.

UNCOLORED THOUGHTS

First edition. June 22, 2023.

ISBN: 979-8223191483

Written by Dr. Sulabh Kumar Shrestha.

Table of Contents

MYTHOLOGIES

When Kalki Met Shiva

"God is dead", the mortals said
        Wings of adharma wide outspread
Kali in vertex, light at the edge
Conscience perished, no saint or sage
Soot skin and atrocious stench
Shiva tandavs as his wraths aflame
In his white horse, the Kalki came
Bowing down, for mercy he begged
Promised the order would reinstate
Shiva said, "you're late, please forsake;
I shall destroy what I create"
And in no time his third eye gaped
From his eye, a fiery flame escaped
In equivalence, energy and weight
Sons of the sun, to the earth they head
Watching the skies before their death
The mortals said, "god is not dead"

Ravana

Ten heads and twenty eyes
    And a love at the first sight
Tenfold dreams, sleepless thoughts
Wandering midst love and lust
Tenfold gloom and desires
Kingdom of despair on fire
Laid upon her beauty
Grows me weak but not guilty
I quit morality
Nectared immortality
Defenseless navel
The seventh day of battle
Still, I wait, Still I wait
For arrows to penetrate
And free myself from her
From one hell to another

Golden Deer

Dreams gilded
　　Like fleeing deer
A fleeting moment
Temptation and fear
Chased all along
Arrow upon its chest
An illusion revealed
But I'm lost in forest

Narcissus

Unrequited love for a heartless being
        The curse of Nemesis never bothered me
But these cold waters did burn like flames
In me with the desires for an unattainable
Own reflections for a mirrorless being
The beauty of others never bothered me
But these cold waters did burn like flames
In me with the desires for an unattainable
And what was in those calm silver waters
I gazed as my chest fluttered and I faltered
Paralyzed gaze gazed in awe of his beauty
And those calm waters gazed back endlessly
He would wane with ripples of my embrace
Sun would rise and set on the water's edge
And last tear fell as my breath became air
What grew upon my chest was Echo's tears
Aeon passed, does this lake remember me,
When she sees me on her coast in spring?
Blooming pale posing flowers on her edge
Was once a man who gazed her for days

Medusa

What I see with fury
    Must turn into a stone
Or though I feel it's beauty
My eyes cannot atone
May I not turn a blind eye
And find no solace in tears
But my soul is petrified
Numb cold to feel or care
The serpent hair I've grown
Should keep you away from me
Or in my garden of stones
Lifeless like me, you shall be
Mirror, should I look at you,
Each day to keep me petrified?
Too keep your sins as my virtues
From solicitude, I must forever hide

Icarus

Fire above, water below
    Ascending to the skies
Vainglory over fear
Fondness for altitudes
Desire to embrace the sun
Allure of the love forbidden
On feathers of hubris
Winged with delusions
Oblivious to the fate
Soaring high like an eagle
Eager gaze towards sun
Befriended by nemesis within
Beauty of the unattainable
Burns the hand reaching
Wings melt, feathers fall
Once fiery, now eyes mirror void
I'm languished near the sun
A moment of silent mourn
Faling down... falling down
Into the seas of despair
Will it save me or drown?

Nemesis of the Sun

The last gaze from the earth to skies
    That burning sun before my eyes
The thing that scorched my sun
But burning brighter than the sun
The fire of vengeance within me
Carrying the wind and the seas
Carrying the hurricane and the rain
To you I shall fly, I shall fly again
Will you be smothered or will I burn?
Whether darkness falls or whether I fall
In afterburn peace, my heart shall cease
I am Daedalus, I am your nemesis...

MEDICINE

At the Gates

Fading into white noise
    Digitized heart steadies
Visions of tunnel light
Plastic windpipes in accord
Oneirophrenia to dreams
White morphine clouds
Rid myself of all diseases
A sweet sighful breeze
Reminiscence of past life
Or a clairvoyance of afterlife
I wake up at the gates
Bedridden between life and death

Journey

Amidst blinding white light in silence
I was slowly turning numb and senseless
But her beckoning voice kept calling my name
Then waving goodbye, out of body I came
There, I saw myself gasping from breath
Caught somewhere between life and death
At the end of a dark road, I saw her face
Passed through the gates, reached for her embrace
The land where nothing ever withered
Serene sounds of rippling clear river
Arches of rainbow, mountains capped with snow
Eternal flowers blooming in celestial meadows
A tender lullaby she sang me to sleep
In a distance, I could hear my heart beep
Dream or reality? My eyes opened wide
For this time, I had survived...

Covid I – Welcome to my RNA

My capricious little genome
    Walking through your ribosomes
Millions of crowned copies
Commandeering your body
A violent storm of cytokine
Blindly destroying everything

Covid II – Thin Air

Fahrenheits rising, magmatic skin
    Gasping for air, breaths machined
Havoc beeping of a life struggling
And slowly as my air gets thin
Dreaming over clouds of morphine
But in dark, I see a silver lining

Covid III - Oxygen

They're drowning in air
    Breathing in despair
Aluminum bottled lives
Keeps them alive
Every minute in litres
Needs needle in meter

Covid IV – We Can't Play Gods

Gowned, we've come for rounds
    Your lungs like deep drowned
A frosted glass ground
Oxyhemoglobin falls down
But nothing we have can cure
Like an alchemist with no elixir

PERSONIFICATION

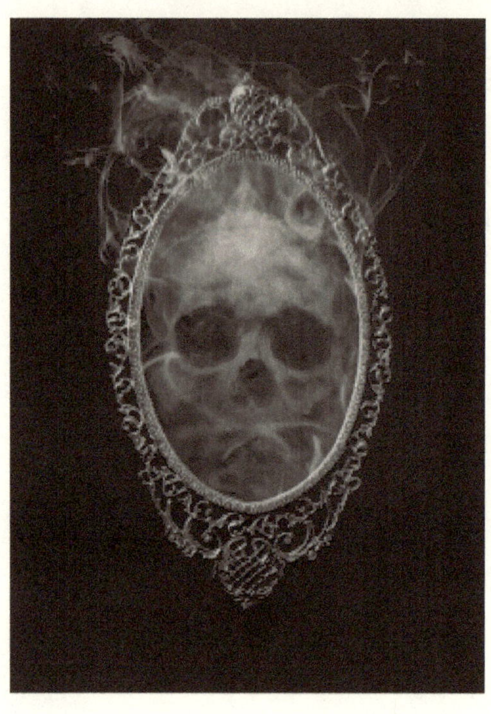

Bullet

Anti-sublimated fire
    Within aegis of metal skin
A caged wanderlust
Waiting to be unshackled
I know my fate
Once I fly, I die
But I'm born to travel
Overriding the speed of sound
My freedom yell
When I escape from chamber
Leaving an invisible trail
Aroma of burnt charcoal
Slowly into your skin
Leaving a swansong tattoo
Through cages of your ribs
Into a chamber of your heart
A beautiful guilt
With red stains on me
I have found meaning of life
That is to die together with you

Mina

Do you believe in life after death?
          Mina... my beloved Elizabeth
I've crossed oceans of time alone
To find you, forever seemedn't long
This Vlad has renounced the cross
This Vlad has lived with a curse
Blood is the life, I lived on the blood
This Vlad once fought for the traitor god.
Away from sunshine that never was mine
Together we'll fade from chains of time
Our love is a fairy tale from eternity
Ov beauty the you and beast the me
Transylvanian light, dethrone the light
Howls in air, on this necromantic rite
Mina, surrender thyself into my embrace
Consent my canines to carve your neck
Suffice my lust, quench my bloodthirst
Taste my blood, inherit my curse
Away from sunshine that never was mine
Together we'll fade from chains of time

Heart Collector

What must I feel with a hollow chest,
    Tearless eyes and a smileless face?
But could these be a mask to hide,
All my pathos and the silent cries?
The night is sunless and so are men
City is sombre, crushed with burden
I'll collect the hearts to ease their pain
And tonight, I shall feel once again

Mirror and the Countess

Oh, my mirror, the beauty beholder
          Days pass by a blink as I hold her
There's a belle in a mentieka lined by fur
I'd kiss her in the mirror, my beloved lover
And only if you could spot a line on her face
I'd tell you how young she looks for her age
Eyeing snow skin, I lie enthralled and dazed
That lusterless diamond encircling her neck
Slowly with grace, as she takes off her crown
Her braided hairs gradient from black to brown
Beneath flawless skin, a sin buried deep down
Unaware of her secrets, they all would drown
In her eyes, the color of mysterious blue skies
In her lips, the stain of vicious red lies
Within castle walls, have disappeared all cries
The valiant blood countess in beautiful disguise
Fear of aging beauty, obsessing her thought
An irresistible lust for the virgin's blood
She is the me – Transylvanian countess of blood
For elixir of youth, we abandoned our god

To Boddah

B orn as a pisces sun
    Feeling too much then none
The dead fear no death
But for my destined fade
I wishn't this fame
Senses lulled with cocaine
Pointing myself, a gun
My unbridled desire to burn

This Is How I Disappeared

I wrote that I would rest eternally
   Into these cold, deep rivers
But they were a bit too shallow
For my thoughts that drowned me forever
I kept walking to the otherside
Until I escaped my memories
A new name at a new place
A new life in time and space
I've disremembered who I was
And the bridge I've crossed
This is how I disappeared

AMBIGUOUS

Temple Bells

When in guilt of sins, my heart swells
      I reach again to ring the temple bells
A silent confession bowing low before his feet
Entering as a beast, returning as a priest
Amnesia in a blink, all sins undone
And on horizon, as a new day dawn
The angel has again fallen from grace
Devouring and being devoured by darkness
And with bloodstains of someone's innocence
I reach again to ring the temple bells

Paperboat

All the memories kept pouring down as words
    Tears drop down, ink blots and paper bloats
A gentle caress to smudge everything I wrote
And I crease, fold, refold it into a paperboat
This letter I wrote, with love to my ghost
A final kiss, goodbye before she begins to float
And as I smile and wave my hands to her
Every moment, she rows away a farther
Rumbling dark clouds above unlocks rain
Struggles a few distance, tumbles again and again
Disappears to infinity with the setting sun
The clockwaves promise – she'd never return
I move on... I move on...

Paperplane

A paper plane on the sky
    How far would it fly?
Passenged by my thoughts
Would a breath keep it alive?
I know it's just a hope
A millionth time redesigned
Destination is never reached
But it's the hope that never dies

What am I?

I am the riddle
     I can't decipher
I am the middle
Of a place nowhere
I am the dream
Of a reality sleeping
I am the scream
Of an aphonic weeping
I am the lake
Rippling on a desert
I am the breath
Exhaled by dead heart
I am the riddle
I can't decipher
What am I?
What am I?
I am nothing

Dissociated

And from coveted serene sleep I woke
    What am I, like a flurry soft smoke?
Like a helium in air, rising slowly above
From threads of my body like a kite cut off
And I watch below on earth I'm still asleep
While I float through the skies blue and deep
Is it the body that keeps me or the body I keep?
It calls me back in but for now I must leave

Chrysalis

"I shall now sleep"
        Said the caterpillar covering
See him not inside
As he's silently mouldering
"Nothing ever dies"
Said the chrysalis breaking
Even so the wings unfurl
He remembers his crawling
"We shall meet again"
Said the butterfly flying
One day we all shed old skin
With the memories undying

Abandoned House

I am grey, I am dark
    The abandoned house
  The loudest silence
  And musty smell
  Fills the air around
  Stagnant for years
  Light bulbs are dead
  Like my dreams
  Windowpane are dusty
  Like my memories
  Come fill me up
  I'm the abandoned house

Coal and Fire

The coal yearns for fire
    Even when burning together
Is there any feeling worse
Than the nostalgia of future?
You are the burning flames
Destined to extinguish
I am the dying embers
Turning into ashes
Never to burn again...
Never to burn again...

Allegory of the Cave

I was born in a cave and caged till date
    A supposed sun in the darkness innate
The truth has been but the shadows I've seen
And all that I've seen is all that I dream
I then climbed out and gazed your sun
Is it or the fire in cave an illusion?
Too bright it's light, blinded my vision
This world is mundane, I must return
In my cave, there's a world I've made
Though be dark, that's where I feel safe
I refuse to be your reality's slave
Refuse to see behind three walls of cave

The Moth and the Flame

The moth knows not why
       But is lured to the flames
His wings driven by his heart
Which belongs to the flames
Burning passionately high
Like the skies in the dusk
Could show him the way
Or burn him to dust

Chronophobia

The hands of time kept moving
 Dirking the dreamers dead
The sands of time kept flowing
Burying the dreamer's beneath
We live in fear, we are distraught
He must be stopped, so I thought
I pulled the jagged dagger out
Stabbed and ripped his heart out
Suddenly, the earth stopped turning
Winds not blowing, rivers not flowing
Everything once in motion
Now frozen with the time
Once my beating heart
Once my breathing lungs
And the blood in my veins
Lied still with the time I killed

Dream Collector

Your dewinged dreams
    Like featherless birds fallen
But shall never die
For I collect and keep
Until their wings regrow
And fly back to your heart

A Half Year Long Night Skies

I gazed at a half year long night skies
    Same were the stars, never did sun rise
Grey was my soul, black was the world
Cold was the world, colder was my soul
Why wouldn't the day divide this night?
I wondered gazing static stars in the skies
What had I done? What had I done?
Remembered I had stopped the earth's rotation
For I was afraid of my countless todays
Rapidly turning into piffling yesterdays

Otherside

The warmth of sunshine after rain
Touches the fogged windowpane
Evaporates the shroud of condensation
And redeems my curious imagination
Feeling lost again as I'm able to see
The world otherside – strange and eerie
But I'll walk out and begin the journey
To conquer all that's written for me
Nostalgia may accompany memories
But soon here, I'll find myself happy
As the strange faces begin to get familiar
On the otherside, I'll carry memories of here

Shedding Skin

The dead skin I'm in
    A disease I'm used to
The insensate comfort
I'm holding on for years
Hoping for its revival
Now I know I must leave
And as I shed my skin
I'm delicate inside
Should I go back in,
Or should I leave it behind?

Midas Touch

Should I touch myself?
    For my heart is cold
And if I touch myself
Will my heart be of gold?
Or to a stone I shall morph
All I touch turns to gold
God, thy boon be a curse
For my soul I once sold

Escapist

All these years, I've only faced
    All the things, I couldn't escape
And all that have once bothered me
I've turned my back and refused to see
Wish they'd vanish but cling to stay
Though they chase, I push them away
Until their shadows grow bigger than me
And shove me down... still I refuse to see
I'd retaliate not, rather leap to sleep
Evaporate into dreams to be concealed
All these years, I've only faced
All the things, I couldn't escape
And when in air, I couldn't breathe
I'd plunge myself into the water beneath

I built a ladder to the sky

Breath
These breath
Hanging by a thread
Cannot I take for granted
With each breath, higher I tread
However bright, even the stars they die
Though I cry, though I try, though I deny
From astute Yama's eye, to hide, who am I?
So, I've built a golden ladder to the sky
Where clouds walk and angels fly
The moon sings her lullaby
'Til ashen be my fire
I climb higher
& higher

NATURE

Sun, Moon, Earth and I

Never could I be the sun
That kept itself burning
To shed light upon others
And not a beam for himself
Never could I be the moon
That kept flaunting her flaws
Had no light of her own
Yet the beauty was uncontested
Never could I be the earth
That loved all whole heartedly
Trees, animals and all the born
And never asked anything in return
I was a mere human being
That never let the light into my heart
That never appreciated beautiful flaws
And the beast that ate the earth

When the Clouds Cry Rain

Thoughts sail like clouds
    On the skyful infinite mind
So many where to travel
But stays above our head
Not so distant to be felt
But still out of our reach
They fall and touch you
When the clouds cry rain
And move somewhere away
Where do these clouds go?
Do they vanish into the air
With afterburn of the sun
Or do they move sideways
Where who needs them most?
To heal their wounded soul
When the clouds cry rain

Autumn in Me

Though they be dear
    Though their allure
That's dead must leave
Like autumn leaves
From their loving trees
Fluttering in breeze
Wintered we both be
The tree and the me
Waiting for the summer
To bud a new another

Smog

The smog fostered in hearts
    Leaked and wrapped the city
Smothered the light and warmth
Long vanished from within us
And no wind blew to carry it away
No rain fell down to wash it away
No tears fell to dwindle it down
This dyspnogenic malevolent smog
Trapped between the mountains
And growing into our hourglass lives
Can find no way out to escape
So slowly wafts back to our hearts

Wind

When will it touch you
  And where will it go?
What can cage it?
Nobody knows...
When will it breeze
And when will it grow
To storm and tornado?
Nobody knows...
She was a wind
And I was a hollow
What she howled?
Nobody knows...

Jacaranda Tree

The fallen blue Jacaranda flowers
    Once fragrant but fragile
Stepped and smeared on ground
Are just the memories
Of beauty and the spring
And reminiscent of the art
The art of living and losing
Of the old lone Jacaranda tree
Standing tall through the seasons
The seasons of constant change

May

May is all purple and cold
    The flowers the trees hold
And all the flowers downed
On the wet tarred ground
All day long, the clouds weep
Birds they sweetly sing and chirp
Air smells of a road tea brew
And the sky is clear and blue

LOVE AND DEATH

Lovesick

She stares with her glass eyes
  She lies silent and paralyzed
She is made of organs of rags
Maquillage of plaster and wax
Tangled with ligamentized wire
Dressed in her bridal attire
Such ashen beauty unearthed
Laid with black roses on bed
With her, he dances and talks
Clocks on the wall anticlocks
Ephemerality of life defied
Love smells like formaldehyde
Elena and Carl forever tied
This kind of love never dies

Funeral Pyre

By the riverside, pale and serene
     On a bed of logs, I am asleep
He chants me a holy hymn
In grief, the loved ones weep
See me, into ashes I am turning
Blinding smoke clouding the air
Aroma of flesh and woods burning
Remember me... once I lived here
Unchained myself from terrene desires
Am I rising beyond life and death?
To heaven or hell? Or a deadend pyre?
Afterlife or oblivion? Waiting on the gate...

Unrequited

Drown me deeper into ambivalent seas
An allure of that cannot be reached
Like the moon in the night skies
The blue hour before the sun rise
I gaze her beauty from a distance
And wish for her in sheer silence
Sands keep falling through hourglass
I wait forever in silence, alas...

ATR-72

Voracious clouds wait impatiently
    To feast upon their dreams
Before they're charred unidentifiable
Like papers burnt to ashes
What defies gravity does enthrall
But that flies must fear the fall
Tons of smoke the gorge hurled
Wish it was from a paper plane

Bridge

He waits on the river's brink
    Dead winter leaves scattered
Hovers the evergrey clouds
Over the sun that radiates life
She stands on the otherside
Both searching for the bridge
That river they wish to cross
Between shores of life and death

2

About the Author

I'm an Orthopedic surgeon from Nepal who loves writing and music. I started writing on Instagram as "quillyporcupine" and have gathered the poems and courage to publish it here.